NEATH AND PORT TALBOT

Yesterdays

NEATH AND PORT TALBOT *Yesterdays*

by David Roberts

Courier

First published in Great Britain in 2004 by
Bryngold Books Ltd.,
Golden Oaks, 98 Brynau Wood, Cimla,
Neath, South Wales, SA11 3YQ.

ISBN 0 9547859 1 6

Printed in Wales by
Dinefwr Press, Rawlings Road,
Llandybie, Carmarthenshire, SA18 3YD.

Contents

An appreciation

Neath and Port Talbot Yesterdays would not have been made possible without the valued assistance of the many residents of Neath and Port Talbot, past and present, who so willingly submitted their own cherished personal photographs of days gone by. However small their individual contribution it is just as important in making this a book that is for the people of the two towns – and by them.
Particular thanks for their assistance are due to:
Cheryl Roberts,
John Newman, Peter Soderstrom,
Roger and Annette Gale, Bryn Thomas,
Mark and Margaret Lemon, Catherine Davies,
Graham and Diane Gilbert,
Colin and Jean Griffiths,
Mike and Val Davies,
Keith and Anne Davies,
Gaynor Hicks, Mary Roberts,
Brian King, Anne George,
Jenny Lewis, Mr G Issac,
Gaynor John, Stanley Pope,
Jeff and Joyce Thomas, Eric Aldum,
Norman and Winifred Reed,
Robert Ball, Simmonds Aerofilms
John Southard, John Vivian Hughes, Colin Scott,
Tony Crocker, Emyr Nicholas and staff at Dinefwr Press

For details of how you can play a part in this valuable ongoing pictorial archive telephone 01639 643961. All photographs offered for the next publication will be welcomed and returned after use.

FOREWORD

SINCE he started the series, David Roberts's fascinating picture books have become a firm favourite with local history lovers. This latest volume will once again delight and inform his readers in equal measures.

While faces and places may have changed through the years, the enduring spirit of the proud towns of Neath and Port Talbot has remained constant and it is that spirit which Neath and Port Talbot Yesterdays celebrates.

David has once again brought together a fascinating collection of images capturing the life of the two towns through so many decades of change.

The Evening Post applauds this achievement, and is delighted to be associated with the latest in this excellent series.

Spencer Feeney
Editor
South Wales Evening Post

KEEPING PACE AND MEETING DEMANDS

Few observers would doubt that in the 21st Century the pace of change is faster than at almost any time before, and nowhere is that more evident than in Neath and Port Talbot.

Both towns, now long united within one county borough, are being re-shaped on many fronts to meet the challenge and demands of the future.

Looking around it is difficult to avoid noticing the way in which many of these changes are manifesting themselves: new homes, new stores, new roads and new industries are all leaving an indelible mark on the area.

New people too, can play a part in this continual reshaping, but then that has long been the case. The written history of Neath and Port Talbot shows clearly that comings and goings have been frequent through their existence.

Today the population of the County Borough of Neath Port Talbot is around 135,000. Those among that figure whose association stretches back down the decades will understand the way things were, but value this opportunity to refresh their memory. Younger and newer inhabitants on the other hand will perhaps appreciate Neath and Port Talbot Yesterdays more as a social guide to years gone by.

There are many routes to the history of Neath and Port Talbot, the pictures contained within the following pages – a people's self portrait – will once again bring colour to the words and add significantly to the framework they construct.

David Roberts, 2004.

Town Times

High Street, Aberafan in the early 1900s. Today the entrance to the Aberafan Shopping Centre is approximately in the centre of this picture. Here though, the Walnut Tree Hotel dominates the scene.

The ivy-clad ruins of Neath Castle fronted by pleasant lawned grounds, early 1900s.

Talbot Street, Aberafan, looking towards Cwmavon, with Jones the printers in the centre, early 1900s.

The Oxford Inn, Windsor Road, Neath, early 1900s. Landlady Margaret Court and her daughter are standing in the doorway.

A view across the rooftops of Aberafan, towards Dinas mountain, 1904. It was probably captured from the tower of St Mary's Church. Today, though some of the terraced housing on the left of the hillside remains, the majority of the other buildings pictured have vanished.

The Square, Neath, looking towards Victoria Gardens, 1905. The Anchor public house on the right is now Milletts store, but the shoe shop on the left is still Stead & Simpsons. Tramlines can be seen running along the centre of the road.

High Street, Aberafan, near its junction with Water Street, presented a busy scene when this 1920s picture was taken.

The Gnoll House and grounds, above Neath town, viewed from the west, 1905.

The former bridge over the River Afan can just be seen in the middle distance of this view of the easternmost extremity of old Aberafan town, early 1920s.

Bungalows overlooking Llantwit Road, Neath, 1920s. The building of houses on the open expanse in front of them means this view would not be possible today.

Traffic waits to enter Station Road, from Bethany Square, in the early 1950s overshadowed by the former Bethany Church. The coach was operated by the firm of Jones Pantdu.

This narrow alleyway, pictured in the mid-1950s, was at the back of Woolworths, Wind Street, Neath. It vanished with a retail redevelopment scheme that gave the company a frontage on Orchard Street.

Orchard Place Baptist Chapel, Orchard Street, Neath, 1955.

A policeman on point duty on the busy pedestrian crossing at the junction of Station Road and Bethany Square, mid-1950s. The building at the end of the road is the Globe Hotel, while the Odeon cinema can be seen on the right.

A policeman stands directing mid-1950s traffic at the town's notorious bottleneck junction between High Street and Water Street which ran between the Walnut Hotel on the left and the Maypole grocery store.

Coronation Road, Neath, renamed Dalton Road, late 1950s.

A United Welsh bus company double decker heads into Neath's Victoria Gardens bus station from Orchard Street, 1960.

Clarence Street, Aberafan, shortly before demolition to make way for town centre redevelopment, 1969.

Port Talbot's central police station, Station Road, late 1960s. It was later replaced with a new police headquarters.

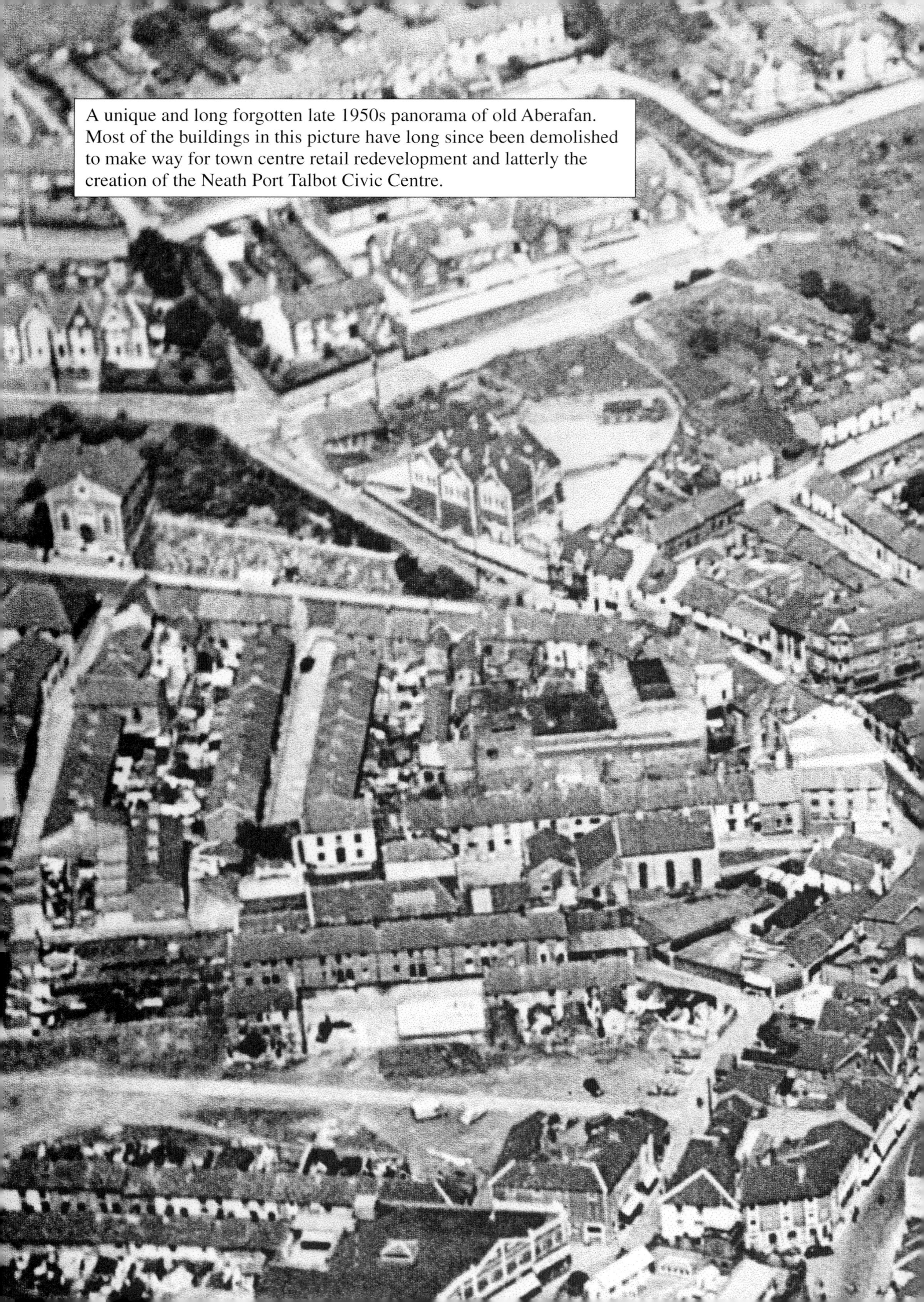

A unique and long forgotten late 1950s panorama of old Aberafan. Most of the buildings in this picture have long since been demolished to make way for town centre retail redevelopment and latterly the creation of the Neath Port Talbot Civic Centre.

Neath's former parks superintendent, Dennis Simpson, stands proudly with representatives of the West Glamorgan Guide movement behind the floral display created by his staff in Victoria Gardens in 1960 to commemorate the golden jubilee of Guiding.

Club owner Bryn Thomas outside his hotel, restaurant and club, Carlton III, Station Road, Port Talbot, the third premises to use that name in the town, mid-1970s.

The inside of the former Wesley Methodist Chapel, London Road, Neath, early 1960s.

Water Street, Aberavon, with the Railway Tavern in the foreground viewed across the main Swansea to Paddington railway line, 1968.

Neath railway station forecourt, early 1960s.

Talbot Square, Aberavon, often referred to as Cwmavon Square, 1973. The Grand Cinema, in High Street, is in the background.

Bridge Street, Neath, mid-1960s. This was the main western traffic gateway to the town at that time.

Traffic flows into and out of Neath along Bridge Street, 1974.

The Grand Hotel, Station Road, Port Talbot, early 1980s.

The Dock Hotel, Port Talbot, early 1980s.

Refurbishment work on the frontage of Currys electrical shop at Orchard Street, Neath in the late 1970s revealed clues to the building's previous use as a public house – The Royal Oak.

Station Road, Port Talbot, before pedestrianisation, January 10, 1986.

The Butchers Arms, Neath, later renamed The Highlander, at the junction of Lewis Road and Eastland Road, early-1980s.

Abbey Road, Port Talbot, after one of the heaviest snowfalls for many years, 1983.

The Halfpenny Bridge across the River Afan, mid-1980s.

Neath Methodist Church, Stockham's Corner, 1983. The road system has altered dramatically since this picture was taken.

The Railway Inn, Bridge Street, Neath, shortly before demolition, 1984.

Windsor Road, Neath, with the town's former police station, on the right, mid-1980s.

A view over the rooftops of Forge Road, Port Talbot with the town centre in the background, 1985.

Melyn Primary School, Mile End Road, Neath shortly before its replacement by a modern building, 1984. Interestingly, Mile End filling station is still displaying prices in both gallons and litres.

Demolition work underway on the Odeon Cinema, Port Talbot, October, 1995.

Gnoll Road Congegational Chapel, Library Road, Neath. Further along building work is underway on the flats and doctors' surgery that replaced Wesley Chapel in London Road, mid-1980s.

The White Hart public house, Neath, presents a lonely picture after all the other buildings around it had been demolished to make way for town centre redevelopment, mid-1980s.

The imposing mock classical façade of the Natwest Bank, Green Street, Neath, 1989. At the time it displayed the bank's former title of National Westminster.

The Corner House café, Station Road, Port Talbot, previously known as Franchi's, mid-1980s.

The building of Safeway's supermarket and car park, Neath, September 1988.

Construction work on Port Talbot Civic Centre, 1985.

The clock tower of St David's Parish Church, dominates this view of Angel Street, Neath, 1988.

Aberavon gasworks, just off Victoria Road, 1985.

Port Talbot in the early 1990s, viewed from the mountainside overlooking the town. This picture confirms just how quickly change can make its mark felt.

FRIENDLY FACES

Members of Cwmavon Ambulance Class, 1911.

What the best dressed people were wearing at Neath weddings, 1929. This picture was taken after the marriage of Harry Cole a butcher in the town's market and his bride Nan John.

A mixed gathering of adults and children, possibly members of the congregation of nearby Graig Chapel, outside Briton Ferry Public Hall, early 1900s.

Friends of the Whist Drive group at Bryn, Port Talbot made a farewell presentation to retiring local GP, Doctor Ryan, 1945.

Members of the congregation of 'little' Bethesda Chapel, Penrhiwtyn, Neath, at their annual Whitsun tea, early 1950s.

Mayor of Neath, Councillor Jack Morgan, headed a group of local dignitaries who handed over cheques for money raised by residents of Neath and District to aid the war effort, during the area's War Weapons Week, February 8, 1941.

Regulars of the Royal Oak pub, Bryn, Port Talbot, at a darts cup presentation, early 1950s.

Men of the congregation of Neath Presbyterian Church, late 1940s. In their midst, the daughter of one of them.

Port Talbot Motor Club members at the presentation evening held following their successful Peter Russek Manuals rally, 1970. The function was held at the Seabank Hotel, Porthcawl.

Committee members of the Gnoll Youth Club, Neath, 1950.

Some of those who attended a presentation evening for recipients of long service awards at the Steel Company of Wales, Port Talbot, 1971.

Former Neath Mayor Len Burton presented a portrait of himself to Melyncrythan Junior School head boy Joey Farmer, while the headteacher and a school colleague look on, early 1950s.

Members of the St John Ambulance Brigade at Skewen, attend a retirement presentation to one of their long serving members, September 1959. The event was held at the group's meeting hall in Dynevor Road.

An officer of the Skewen branch of the St John Ambulance Brigade presents a token in salute to the long service of one of the group's members, 1959.

Mayor of the Borough of Afan, Sylvan Thomas, entertains workmates from the Steel Company of Wales, Port Talbot at the Mayor's parlour, 1976.

Briton Ferry Townswomen's Guild members during a function at the Castle Hotel, Neath, early 1950s.

Residents of Elder Road and Mayberry Road, Baglan, united for a street party to celebrate the Silver Jubilee of Queen Elizabeth II, 1977.

Neath Afternoon Townswomen's Guild in fun and fancy dress mode, 1959.

Mayor of Port Talbot, Mel John, together with Deputy Mayor Jim Warren take centre stage in a gathering of local civic leaders and other dignitaries at the Afan Lido sports centre, 1972.

Some of the guests at a Neath coal merchant's Christmas function, early 1960s.

Employees of the Albion steelworks, Briton Ferry gather for a retirement presentation to one of their colleagues, 1967.

The successful entrant in the Miss Neath competition, together with runners up and judges, 1962. She later represented the town in the Miss Wales Bathing Beauty competition.

Alderman Ernie Molland, pictured between his twin daughters who shared the duties of mayoress for his mayoral year, 1962-63. The picture was taken shortly after the mayor-making ceremony.

Port Talbot Mayor Ted Owen joins in a charity bike ride with other local celebrities in aid of the Tenovus Cancer charity, 1975.

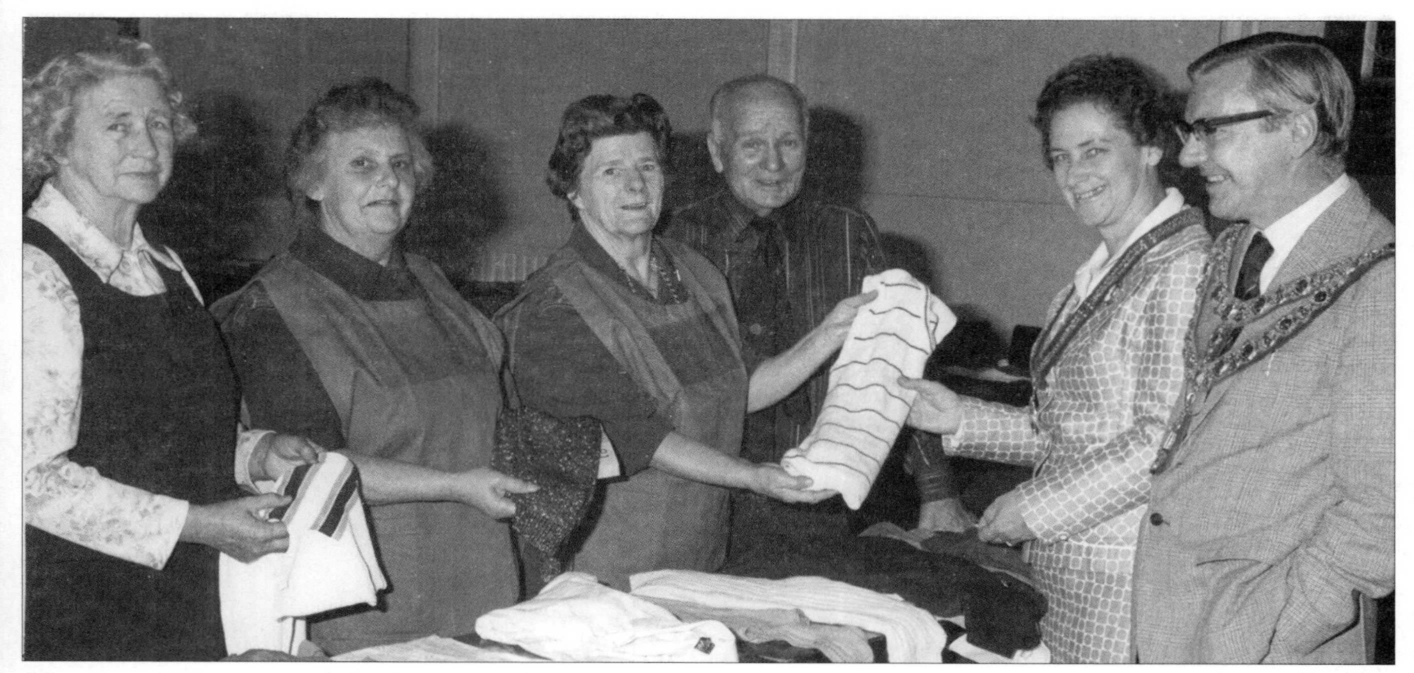

Mayor and Mayoress of the Borough of Afan, Elwyn and Mrs Williams, check out some of the merchandise at a fund raising event held in aid of the mayor's charity, 1979. The event has now been held for around 50 years.

George Preece was a familiar face at Port Talbot flower shows where he successfully exhibited for many years. He is seen here in 1978 with some of his prize blooms.

Successful competitors, organisers and judges at Port Talbot Horticultural Society's annual show, 1983.

Garage and office staff of N&C Luxury Coaches, James Street, Neath on the occasion of the retirement of its engineer Mr Beddoe, 1963. The presentation was made by company electrician David Davies.

Newlyweds pose with their family and fellow guests after their wedding at Briton Ferry Congregational Chapel, 1964.

Crowds came from just about everywhere when song and dance star Frankie Vaughan visited Neath Boys' Club, Melyncrthyan, 1968. The entertainer was a long time supporter of the youth organisation. Just behind Frankie Vaughan is international football referee Clive Thomas.

Employees of Taylor & Sons engineering works, Briton Ferry, on a night out, 1969.

The women's section of Bryn ward Labour Party visting the office of Port Talbot mayor Ted Owen, 1975.

Members of Neath Amateur Operatic Society, early 1970s.

Port Talbot sports star, entertainer, fund-raiser and all-round personality, Bryn Thomas, with the illuminated scroll admitting him as an honorary Freeman of the Borough of Port Talbot, 1990.

Briton Ferry Slimming Club members, early 1970s.

Longford Ladies Club on an outing to Blackpool, 1970s.

Prayers led by Rev Grenfell Rees when Guides, Trefoil members and civic leaders including Mayor of Neath Martin Thomas, gathered at the home of West Glamorgan Guide Commisioner Miss Freda Gibbins to mark the occasion of the Silver Jubilee of Queen Elizabeth II, 1977.

Oscar–winning, Neath-born actor Ray Milland makes one local autograph hunter happy during a visit to the town's Gnoll Primary School which he attended as a youngster, early 1970s.

District Diary

The Evans family outside their home in Morgans Road, Melyncrythan, Neath, 1910. The family ran a successful coal merchant business.

Looking towards Lletty Harry across Ynys Farm, Port Talbot, around 1900.

Caerhendy, Port Talbot, on the hillside overlooking the lower Afan Valley, 1880.

Skewen Post Office, New Road, with a postman in the doorway, one of its white-aproned staff and a customer outside, early 1900s.

The newly-built Cwrt Sart School, Old Road, Briton Ferry, 1929.

What's missing? The sprawling Sandfields housing estate that's what! Oh yes, and the lengthy promenade. The Jersey Beach Hotel stands a lonely sentinel at Aberavon Beach, 1929, with very little hint of a promenade then. In the foreground a coaster is being guided into the mouth of the River Afan towards Port Talbot docks by a pilot boat.

Cunard Terrace, Cwmavon, with the police station on the left, looking up the Afan Valley, 1910.

New Road, Skewen, early 1930s.

Ynys and Rhyslyn, Pontrhydyfen, with the village's station up on the left hand side, mid-1930s.

A couple, seated right, gaze across Crynant, then with far fewer dwellings, late 1930s.

The bowling green and tennis courts at Pontrhydyfen, late 1930s. The backs of houses in Morgan Terrace can clearly be seen, along with the Port Talbot Railway in the foreground. By then it had been absorbed by GWR.

A fascinating view of Fabian Way, near Jersey Marine. It was taken from the air in 1948 and shows early work on the dual carriageway that was to carry traffic from Neath River bridge into Swansea. The new road was ready some years before the river crossing and scythed through the Swansea Bay Golf Club's course. The 'kink' in the road towards the top right of the picture is interesting. When complete it took a different course here. Today, the Visteon automotive plant is to the top right, alongside the road.

A German Luftwaffe aerial reconnaissance photograph taken over Neath and Port Talbot on January 15, 1941. It shows clearly Briton Ferry in the upper centre, Baglan to the upper right, Baglan Burrows, with its high sand dunes, to the bottom right and Jersey Marine to the bottom left. The River Neath snakes its way down through the centre. Box B, drawn by the Germans in the top left focuses on the swing bridge railway crossing over the river, the one in the centre, Briton Ferry Dock. The photograph was taken just a month before the infamous three Nights' Blitz which flattened the centre of Swansea. This original Luftwaffe photograph – complete with its observation markings – was retrieved from Germany shortly after the end of the Second World War.

Ynys Bowling Green, Velindre, Port Talbot, late 1940s. Ynys Farm buildings can be seen behind. Today, though the bowling green survives, the farm area is the site of the Ynys Y Gored housing development.

This picture was taken at Penshanel, Skewen in the early 1980s. It shows reclamation work, just completed, on the site of William Bater & Sons' Maesmelyn Quarry. Today the site has matured and few hints of the former quarry are visible.

The Mission Hall at Clyne in the Neath Valley, May, 1975.

Dorothy and Vera Howells outside the shop they ran in Ormond Street, Briton Ferry, then called Water Street, early 1950s.

The road behind this young engineer at Baglan Engineering works is the old A48 at Baglan. The works was demolished in the 1950s to make way for the dual carriageway that exists today. This picture was taken in 1951.

The main walkway at Vivian Park, Aberavon, 1949.

Construction work on the Neath by-pass, March 1951. This is the site of Briton Ferry roundabout. Briton Ferry viaduct is on the upper left and McDonalds burger bar is now on the site at the bottom right.

Castle Drive, Cimla, Neath, after a heavy snowfall, 1983.

Hanging out the washing on the pre-fab development at Farm Drive, Sandfields, Port Talbot, 1952.

The Tower Hotel, Jersey Marine, with the road alongside through the village almost obliterated by heavy snow, 1983.

The Baglan Engineering Company's works, on the left, at its original site at Baglan, 1952. It later relocated to Melyncrythan, Neath to allow for the construction of the A48 dual carriageway between Briton Ferry roundabout and Sunnycroft roundabout.

A view across Skewen, early 1980s. The Oakhill Park housing development was later built on this site.

The viaduct at Pontrhydyfen, early 1960s.

The ruins of Neath Abbey, with the Tennant Canal alongside, 1984.

This car came to grief when it rolled off the road into the garden of a house at Castle Drive, Cimla, early 1980s.

Baglan from the air, August 1961. The picture was taken by airman Gordon Wilson from an RAF Canberra bomber on a flight to photograph Neath River bridge.

Flats at The Saltings, Briton Ferry, 1984.

Industrial development at the Ynys, Velindre, Port Talbot, late 1970s. It included construction company Andrew Scott's Rutherglen works and in the centre, Marcroft wagon repair depot. Today this is the site of the Ynys Y Gored housing development.

Part of the scattered hillside community at Mount Pleasant, Cymmer, 1980.

Wildbrook housing development, Taibach, Port Talbot, blanketed by snow, 1982.

The Ivy Tower, on the hillside above Tonna, Neath, 1984.

A huge pall of smoke hangs over blazing Dinas Mountain, Baglan, viewed from Baglan Moors, April 1984.

Ynysygwas bridge, Cwmavon, which collapsed after heavy rain turned the River Afan into a raging torrent, 1985. It was later replaced by a new crossing.

Dyffryn Chapel, Ffrydwyllt Street, Taibach, 1986.

Demolition work underway on the flats at Hengwrt, Briton Ferry, December, 1985.

The building that was once the civic headquarters of Margam Urban District Council, still retains its architectural splendour, October, 1985.

Parties and Processions

Members of Glamorgan Constabulary provide a guard of honour following a civic service at Orchard Place Baptist Church, Neath, for the town's first citizen, 1937. Pictured centre, is the mayor, Cecil Hedge, and on his right, his deputy, Ned Hutchinson.

A Whitsun parade wends its way down Pentyla and through High Street, Aberavon, early 1900s.

Station Road, Port Talbot was the scene of this early 1900s procession, which included horse-drawn carts, an early car and even, behind that, someone wheeling their bicycle.

Members of Siloh Church are at the front of this Whitsun procession, pictured making its way along Windsor Road, near its junction with Florence Street, Neath, 1910.

Residents of Morgans Terrace, Pontrhydyfen at their celebrations to mark the Coronation of King George VI, 1937.

Old Henry Streeet, Neath was a hive of activity when residents held a street party to celebrate the Coronation of King George VI, 1937.

These were some of the friends who turned up for the birthday party of Gareth Trott at Bryn Road, Neath, 1949.

Children of Undeb Row, Cwmavon, at the street party organised by their parents to celebrate the Coronation of Queen Elizabeth II, June 1953.

Staff of Marks and Spencer's Neath store at an annual dinner and dance, early 1950s.

Residents of Seaward Avenue, Sandfields, Port Talbot parade in fancy dress during their celebrations to mark the Coronation of Queen Elizabeth II, June 1953.

Guests at a Neath Coal Merchants Association dinner, early 1950s.

Some of the participants in the Whitsun procession held by Neath chapels, make their way down Windsor Road, early 1950s.

The Central Club, London Road, Neath was the venue for a Christmas party held for children of employees of N&C Luxury Coaches, 1952.

Earl Alexander of Tunis unveils the foundation stone of the Afan Lido, June 27, 1963. He later went on to officially open the Evans Bevan playing fields, near Sunnycroft roundabout, Baglan.

Some of the Bryn Road, Neath, residents who organised a party at nearby Mount Pleasant bowling club, to celebrate the Coronation of Queen Elizabeth II , June 1953.

Youngsters of Rugby Avenue, Neath, dressed up to celebrate the Coronation of Queen Elizabeth II, June 1953.

Her Majesty Queen Elizabeth II leaves the Afan Lido on a wet mid-summer's day after declaring the Olympic-sized swimming pool officially open. The Mayor of Port Talbot, James Lewis is on her left, June 25, 1965.

Posing for the camera at Park Street, Neath, during celebrations to mark the Coronation of Queen Elizabeth II, June, 1953.

Contestants in the Miss Fairy and Miss Rosebud competition at Aberavon Beach, with organiser and host 'Uncle' Bryn Thomas, early 1960s.

Llandarcy Insitute was the venue for this dance organised by first year apprentices at BP Llandarcy oil refinery, 1953.

Contestants in a beauty competition at Aberavon Beach, with seaside host Bryn Thomas, late 1960s.

Children aboard the Crynant council pre-fab site float for the carnival held by the village to celebrate the Coronation of Queen Elizabeth II, 1953.

Regulars of Baglan Social Club, Lodge Drive, at a fancy dress evening, 1966.

Members of Neath Amateur Operatic Society let their hair down at a fancy dress dance, 1956.

MEXICO
NO
CHA

Children from Heol Penlan, Longford, Neath, who attended a party at the community's memorial hall, 1957.

Staff of women's outfitters Eileen Beckingham, Neath, at their Christmas party, 1957.

Guests at Pontrhydyfen Rugby Club's annual dinner, 1970.

Guests at a fund raising function held in aid of the Royal National Lifeboat Institution at the Steel Company of Wales canteen, Margam, 1971.

Participants in the annual Whitsun march head along Windsor Road, Neath, towards Stockham's Corner, 1961.

Members of the Marjorie Sanderson School of Dancing, Port Talbot, at a fancy dress party, Christmas 1962.

Miss World and Miss Australia, Belinda Green officially opens the new Seaway Parade depot of hire firm Port Talbot Plant, 1973. The town's Mayor and Mayoress Ivor and Mrs Jones were also in attendance together with company executives.

Residents of Arthur Street, Neath didn't allow a little rain to dampen their spirits during their party to help celebrate the Silver Jubilee of Queen Elizabeth II, 1977.

Staff of Neath General Hospital at their Christmas dinner and dance, 1970.

Employees of Neath Department of Health and Social Security office at a function in the Langland Bay Hotel, Swansea, 1975.

Some of those who attended a Tramps Ball at Baglan Social Club, 1971.

Participants in the annual Whitsun procession at Cwmavon, 1975.

Guests at the staff dance of the Albion works of the Briton Ferry Steel Company, mid-1970s.

Young residents of Castle Drive, Cimla, Neath sit down for their party to celebrate the Coronation of Queen Elizabeth II, 1977.

Members of the choir of St Catherine's Church, Old Road, Melyncrythan, march into Neath's Gnoll rugby ground, the destination of the annual Whitsun procession, early 1980s. A united service followed the assembly there.

Retail Roundup

The Gwalia boys' clothier, gents outfitters and hatters of M H Daniels at 23 Green Street, Neath, 1905.

Lewis's sports accessory shop, Commercial Road, Taibach, late 1950s.

Staff of Lewis John, saddlery and harness makers outside their shop at The Parade, Neath, opposite the Castle Hotel, 1905.

The Margam Road premises of the Taibach and Port Talbot Co-operative Society, with its butchery store alongside, early 1950s.

The House of Cards, Church Street, Aberavon was just one of a number of shops that occupied premises under and around the former Municipal Buildings at Port Talbot until their demolition to make way for town centre redevelopment. This view which shows one of the entrances to the arcade that contained more shops, was taken in 1970. The Cavendish furniture store, on the left, can be seen boarded up awaiting demolition.

The Williams corner shop, Stanley Road, Skewen, with proprietor Dorothy Williams in the doorway, 1925.

Hopkins tobacconist, on The Square, Neath, with its window crammed with smokers' requisites, mid-1930s. Inside it also stocked stationery and fancy goods. Today Shaw's drapery store occupies the building.

Some of the shops that drew trade to mid-1970s Station Road, Port Talbot.

Staff of grocers Peglers at Queen Street, Neath, take a break from their labours, early 1950s.

The Melada bakers and confectioners, Station Road, Port Talbot, late 1970s. Alongside, The Gem sweet shop and Ray Lewis opticians.

Two views of the Hill Cycle Company shop at the easternmost end of Windsor Road, Neath, February, 1957. The shop was a mecca for cyclists and model railway enthusiasts, as well as stocking a wide range of toys.

Grocer Ken Roberts, behind the counter of his Cambrian Dairy shop, Neath, shortly before it closed its doors for the final time, 1984.

Left empty by the departure of Fine Fare, Port Talbot's first supermarket, this building alongside Bethany Chapel in Station road offered plenty of bargains from the array of stalls that operated under the banner of the Jubilee Shopping Hall, 1985. Today it is a JobCentre.

Station Road, Port Talbot, looking towards Bethany Square, 1985.

Tom Williams and Son, high class fishmongers, Windsor Road, Neath. Alongside fish was also on the menu at the Model chip bar, 1985.

Some of the small stores in Station Road, Port Talbot, 1985.

The E Griffiths' store at Commercial Street, Neath, was one of the town's last traditional family grocers. It is seen here in 1988 shortly before closing down.

Tots and Teens

Granny's turn to baby sit. This toddler was under the closest of supervision in the back garden of his Mansel Street, Port Talbot home, early 1930s.

These two youngsters – William George Blethyn and his sister Mary looked a little apprehensive when they had their picture taken outside the door of their Llewellyn Street, Aberavon home, 1918.

Ready for the off in his pride and joy. This youngster is all set to take to the back lane of Mansel Street, Port Talbot in his new pedal car, mid-1930s.

A Sunday School class at London Road Presbyterian Church, Neath, 1921.

Members of the Young Peoples' Guild at Neath Wesley Church, London Road, during a pageant they performed in 1924. Seated in the centre is the minister, Rev William Cann.

Never mind the Wild West, this young cowboy was snapped at Baglan, mid-1950s.

It was a case of donning Sunday best for these youngsters when the time came to have their picture taken with their parents and grandmother outside their Aberavon home, 1920.

Playing games in the yard of Alderman Davies' School, St David's Street, Neath, 1928.

Girls from Cwmavon Junior School pictured during a mountainside nature ramble, 1957.

Girl Guides from Bryncoch during a ramble on the mountainside at Drummau, Skewen, 1928.

A sandcastle model of Margam Castle, built by a group of landscape gardening students on Aberavon Beach during the summer of 1975. They were taking part in a competition.

Neath Methodist Church Girl's Guildry, 1940.

A concert performed by young members of the Sunday School of Graig Chapel, Lodge Cross, Briton Ferry, 1950.

A determined young girl clambers onto an antiquated three wheeler cycle outside her Baglan home, 1939.

This youngster had been enjoying himself playing on a house-building site near his Sandfields, Port Talbot home, mid-1950s.

These youngsters had taken part in the St David's Day concert at Mountain School, Aberavon, 1955.

Members of the 14th (Neath) Cimla Scout troop, 1955.

Richard Burton was just a budding film star when this picture was taken while he was being interviewed by a BBC reporter at Caradoc Street, Taibach, Port Talbot, surrounded by children, 1953.

Guides and leaders of the 1st Cimla Company camping at Saundersfoot, 1956.

There is always lots to do on Guide camp as these girls of the 1st Bryncoch, Neath Company discovered in 1959.

Neath & District Sea Cadets on parade at their TS Encounter base, Briton Ferry, 1981.

Neath's September Fair always provides a break for young and old as this youngster discovered in 1968.

Meet the lads whose team might have been called Southdown Road United, Sandfields, Port Talbot, in 1961. For that of course is where they all lived.

Five young girls prepare for their first Corpus Christi at St Joseph's RC Junior School, Pendrill Street, Neath, 1980. Shortly after the school moved to a new building at Cook Rees Avenue, Westernmoor.

Mr Entertainment at Aberavon Beach for many years was 'Uncle' Bryn Thomas, pictured here making sure these youngsters all enjoyed their visit to the seaside and had lots of fun, 1960.

Mayor and Mayoress of Neath Councillor and Mrs Martin Thomas with a group of Neath Brownies at Glynfelin, Bryncoch during celebrations to mark the Silver Jubilee of Queen Elizabeth II, July 1977.

Moving Ways

Crowds leave a train at Aberavon Seaside station, intent perhaps on a day at the seafront, early 1920s.

One of the horse-drawn hearse wagons used by cab proprietors and livery stable keepers A E Evans & Co, of 21 & 22 Alfred Street, Neath, 1905.

There were no trains running on the Vale of Neath line at Resolven on December 19, 1911. Serious flooding had brought the waters of the River Neath almost up to platform height.

Gaen's Garage at Talbot Road, Port Talbot, supplied and serviced many of the town's early cars, late 1940s.

The Gaen's Garage recovery truck looks in need of some help itself in the heavy snows of 1947. The former War Department, left hand drive, vehicle is seen struggling to someone's aid at Margam.

The incline at Briton Ferry, early 1920s. As a loaded wagon came down, its weight pulled an empty one back up.

This was how Prime Minister Ramsey McDonald was ferried around the Neath area during a visit in the early 1920s. Alongside him is driver David Ball.

A train draws into Pontrhydyfen railway station, late 1920s.

A train leaves Cymmer Afan station in the Afan Valley, bound for Port Talbot, early 1950s.

Two Neath women – Mrs HelenThompson of Lewis Road and Mrs Bertha Child, of Llewellyn Avenue – pose for a picture alongside their chauffeur-driven Riley car on a countryside jaunt, 1928.

A group of railwaymen pause from their labours outside Neath East signal box while the signalman peers out of his window, 1930s.

This locomotive served its railway masters well in its prime, but here it was being used as a steam generator at Taylor's foundry, Briton Ferry, 1931.

Dyffryn Yard locomotive sheds, near Taibach, Port Talbot, early 1950s

A unique view of Neath River bridge as it snakes its way towards Briton Ferry Dock viaduct, days before opening in the early autumn of 1955. The river crossing, which allowed traffic to by-pass Neath for the first time, and also shortened journeys between Swansea and the east, was then the largest post war civil engineering project undertaken in the United Kingdom.

A Thomas Bros bus makes its way through Sandfields Estate, Port Talbot, early 1950s.

An ECW-bodied Western Welsh Leyland single deck bus awaits its next tour of duty at the company's Neath Abbey garage and yard, mid-1950s.

Station Road, Port Talbot, provides the backdrop for a picture of one of the Thomas Bros Leyland Tiger Cub single deck buses that served the town through the late 1950s and early 1960s.

Looking down the line from Crymlyn Road bridge, Skewen, towards BP Llandarcy oil refinery, mid-1950s.

One of the American built, diesel locomotives used within the Steel Company of Wales, Port Talbot, early 1960s.

A South Wales Transport AEC Renown double decker pictured at Orchard Street, Neath,1960s.

These two Bristol open-top double deckers ferried thousands of passengers to and from the seafront at Aberavon Beach during the 1960s.

A South Wales Transport AEC Regent III double decker heads into Victoria Gardens bus station, Neath, on its way from Swansea to Margam, early 1960s.

The old and the new – two types of buses used by Port Talbot operator Thomas Bros pictured heading along Victoria Road, Aberavon, mid-1960s.

The purpose-built N&C Luxury Coach company's garage and workshops just off Briton Ferry roundabout, mid-1960s. It later became a transport depot for Calor Gas and latterly the base for Swansea Car Auctions.

The driver of the last train to run on the Neath Valley line, before it was mothballed for many years, hands over his single line operating token to the signalman at Neath Riverside box, 1970s.

Cwmavon railway station, March 1963.

South Wales Evening Post Journalist Tony Crocker watches the first 100,000 tonnes iron ore carrier berth safely in Port Talbot tidal harbour, August 1968.

Two timber boats at Port Talbot docks, early 1970s.

A Castle class locomotive, followed by a Hall class, at Neath locomotive sheds, early 1960s.

Neath motorcyclist Roger Gale, with his pride and joy – a Royal Enfield 350 Bullet machine, 1968.

N&C Luxury coach TWN 557 looks a sorry site at the company's Briton Ferry depot after a serious collision at Cardiff, 1968.

The Port Talbot Docks pilot vessel Margam Abbey in the estuary of the River Afan, May 1984.

Horsepower was still the preferred power option for this rag and bone collector seen near Port Talbot Docks, 1984.

Mini buses were the order of the day at Victoria Gardens, Neath by the mid-1980s.

School Spotlight

Some of the pupils of Alderman Davies' Girls School, Neath, with teacher Miss Thomas, 1911.

Form 5b at Port Talbot County School, 1942, with their teacher and headteacher.

Pupils of Creunant Junior School prepare for a Christmas production, 1925.

Standard 2, Vernon Place Council School, Briton Ferry, 1929.

Mrs Jones' class at Baglan Junior School, 1962.

Standard 5, Vernon Place Council School, Briton Ferry, 1929.

Pupils of Central School, Port Talbot, 1953.

Some of the pupils of Clyne School, Neath, with their teacher and headteacher, early 1950s.

A class at Gnoll Junior School, Neath, 1954.

These children at Baglan Infants School were dressed in traditional Welsh costume to celebrate St David's Day, 1965.

These children of Cimla Infants School were taken out onto Cimla Common to have their picture taken, 1956.

A lesson in knitting seemed to be the order of the day for these girls at Coedffranc Girls School, 1956.

A party of pupils from Heathmont High School, Pentyla, Port Talbot all set for a trip to Paris when this picture was taken in June 1965.

Pupils who attended Neath Boys Grammar School, 1956.

Gnoll Secondary Modern School dance group, 1958 with teacher Reg Teale.

A class at Glanafan Comprehensive School, Port Talbot, 1966.

Standard 5b, Alderman Davies' Boys' School, 1958.

A class at Baglan Junior Mixed School, 1966, with teacher Mrs Griffiths.

Some of the girls who attended Alderman Davies' Girls School, Neath, 1960.

Form 1b, Glanafan Comprehensive School, 1969 with their teacher Mrs E Fowler.

Some of the students and lecturers from one of the departments at Neath Technical College, 1961.

Form 4b, Baglan Junior School, 1972 with their teacher Mr L Lloyd.

Form 2a, Neath Boys' Grammar School, January 30, 1961.

Teacher D R Taylor with form 1t, Glanafan Comprehensive School, Port Talbot, 1973.

Dressed to celebrate St David's Day – a class at Tonna Infants School, 1966.

Prefects at Rhydhir Secondary Modern School, Longford, Neath Abbey, 1965.

Form 6a2, Glanafan Comprehensive School, May 1980 with teacher Tom Davies and head teacher I R Davies.

A class at Cimla Infants School, Neath, late 1960s.

Music was on the minds of these pupils at Pontrhydyfen Primary School, 1975. Head teacher Stanley Jones is at the back.

Prefects and some of the teachers at Glanafan Comprehensive School, June 1980.

Some of the children at Hengwrt Primary School, Briton Ferry, St David's Day, 1972.

Form 5k, Dyffryn Comprehensive School, Port Talbot, 1980.

Class 3, St Joseph's On The Hill Primary School, Westernmoor Road, Neath, 1980.

Auntie Wendy's Playgroup, who met at the old church hall, Cimla Common, Neath, 1984.

Form 1k Cefn Saeson Comprehensive School, Cimla, Neath, 1982.

The reception class at Central Infants School, Port Talbot, March 1983.

Form 4g Dyffryn Comprehensive School, Port Talbot 1980.

A group of pupils who attended Cefn Saeson Comprehensive School, Cimla, Neath, with teacher Mrs Parry, 1987.

WORKING AT IT

Melyn Tinplate Works employees, early 1900s.

A pickling and annealing gang at Baglan Bay Tinplate Works, 1909.

Hauliers at Cwrt-Y-Betws Colliery, 1913. It was sited on land near the Glamorgan Sports Club at Llandarcy. The colliery began operating 1888 and closed just a year after this picture was taken.

Some of the teaching staff at Crynant Primary School, early 1920s.

Some of the men who worked at Port Talbot Central Station, early 1920s.

A construction group from the Great Western Railway's engineering department at Neath, August 1922.

Employees of the Melyn tinplate works, Neath, 1929.

Police Sergeant Joseph King, of Whittington Street police station, Tonna, Neath, with his wife Louise, 1930s.

Gaen's Garage, Talbot Road, Port Talbot, late 1940s, where much of the servicing requirements of the town's motorists was met.

Bater Brothers' Maesmelyn Quarry, Penshanel, Skewen, 1930s.

Workers at the Japan works, Melyncrythan, Neath, 1940.

Baglan Engineering Company at its original site near Swan Street, Baglan, July 1952. These buildings were later demolished and the works relocated to Melyncrythan, Neath, to allow for the construction of the A48 dual carriageway from Briton Ferry roundabout to Sunnycroft roundabout, Baglan.

Mrs Bertha Child, right, with colleagues at the Civil Defence station in Dwryfelin Road, Neath, during the Second World War, 1942.

Employees of Neath Corporation Gas Works, Millands Road, Neath, 1946.

Marcroft Wagon Repairs staff at Margam sidings, 1957.

Staff of the North canteen at the Steel Company of Wales, Margam, 1952.

Construction of new foundations and extra supports for the welding and fabrication shop at Baglan Engineering Company works, March, 1953. The work was carried out by Andrew Scott. Foreman Bill Ray is standing supervising the work.

Wagon repairers at Marcroft works, Velindre, Port Talbot, 1957.

These two women provided newspapers, books and magazines for rail travellers from the W H Smith stand on Neath Railway Station, early 1950s.

Pouring molten metal into moulds at the casting shop of Dynevor Engineering works, Neath, 1954.

A lathe operator at Cam Gears automotive plant at Resolven, 1960.

Port Talbot Borough Council workers at its Morrison Road yard, behind the shopping centre, 1960.

The design and pattern-making shop at the Baglan Engineering Company, Melyncrythan, Neath, late 1950s.

The foundry at the Baglan Engineering Company's works, Melyncrythan, Neath, late 1950s.

Training centre staff and apprentices at the Metal Box factory, Neath, 1959.

Staff of Port Talbot Borough Council's treasurer's department at the Old Vicarage headquarters, May 1967 with the mayor William Lewis.

Workers at Dynevor Engineering Company, Neath, enjoy an after work celebration, 1960.

One of a pair of AEC Regent III double decker buses used by Port Talbot Borough Council's housing maintenance section as mobile workshops and canteens. The vehicles were previously owned by South Wales Transport. This one is pictured in 1969.

Three of the volunteers who gave up their time to build Cimla Gospel Hall, behind the Cimla Hotel – Minister Alan Jenkins, Mr Tucker and Albert Thomas, October, 1961.

Neath coal merchants Bernard Davies, of Ivor Davies & Son, left, and Donald Heggie, after both were presented with a diploma by the Coal Utilisation Council, mid-1960s.

Owners and employees of coal merchants Ivor Davies & Son and C Heggie Ltd., at the coal yard, Neath, with their delivery lorries, mid-1960s.

Neath General Hospital kitchen staff making their 1968 Christmas puddings.

The garage and workshops originally built for the N&C Luxury Coach company at Briton Ferry, had been taken over for use by the Calor Gas company's transport section by 1972.

Three postmen pictured behind Neath General Post Office, 1968.

Blast furnaces one, two and three at the British Steel Corporation's Port Talbot works, 1984.

Staff of Crynallt Junior School, Cimla, Neath, early 1980s.

Smoke and steam reaches skyward at BP Chemicals Baglan Bay plant on a still March evening, 1982.

Line checkers at Cam Gears, Resolven, 1979.

These two bulky loads presented plenty of work for their drivers and those supervising their progress as they head down Station Road, Port Talbot, on their way to the town's steelworks, October, 1985.

The main entrance to BP's Llandarcy oil refinery, 1986.

REST AND PLAY

Miss Freda Gibbins with a party of District Ranger Guides leaving Neath Railway station for two weeks holiday in Switzerland on June 24, 1939. Little did they know then that the start of the Second World War was just weeks away.

A group of men on Aberavon seafront, with the Jersey Beach Hotel, behind, 1909.

A Neath family take a caravan holiday in Oxwich, Gower, 1953.

Three generations sit in the summer sun at Victoria Gardens, Neath, 1954.

On the beach at Aberavon, in front of the Jersey Beach Hotel, 1910.

A group of women from Pontrhydyfen on a day trip to Porthcawl, early 1930s.

An outing of Neath building workers, 1938.

Pupils from Neath Boys' Grammar School on a trip to Norway, 1954.

Members of Neath Wesley Church, London Road, all set to board a coach outside the town's library that would take them on a summer outing, 1950.

Women from the Collins mineral water factory, Briton Ferry, on a trip to Blackpool, early 1950s.

Members of Neath Presbyterian Church on a day's outing, late 1950s

The boating pool on Aberavon seafront with the Bay View Social Club and Sandfields housing estate behind mid 1960s.

Family fun on Aberavon Beach, 1949 – dad was taking this one for the album!

A group of Bryn Senior Citizens, Port Talbot, all set for their annual holiday, 1960.

Women members of Neath Presbyterian Church on their annual day out, late 1950s.

Crowds gather around an event organised by Port Talbot's 'Uncle' Bryn Thomas on Aberavon seafront, mid-1960s.

An N&C luxury coach provided the transport for these Neath railwaymen on a late 1950s outing.

Pupils of Sandfields Comprehensive School in London, 1960. They were on their way to Italy for a holiday.

A group of boys from Melyncrythan, Neath, on holiday in Blackpool, 1961.

Pensioners from Bryn, Port Talbot during a holiday trip to Paignton, Devon, 1966.

Miami Beach Amusement Park, Aberavon, seafront, 1976.

Mayor of Afan, Councillor Sylvan Thomas, presents the prizes after a kite flying competition at Aberavon Beach, 1976.

THE ENTERTAINERS

Briton Ferry Choral Society – winners of the Royal National Eisteddfod of Wales, 1915.

Port Talbot Progressive Club's Chinese jazz band, 1928.

Chorus members of Neath Amateur Operatic Society's production of the musical The Desert Song, 1932.

A musical performance by Cwmavon chapelgoers, 1947.

A Skewen jazz band leads a procession through the village, late 1930s.

The Romany Kids juvenile character jazz band, Briton Ferry, 1937. Its members, pictured with instructor Stan Howells, won many trophies, prizes and cups along with the British chamnpionships that year.

Members of Port Talbot YMCA stage a production of the pantomime Aladdin, 1950.

Pwllyglaw Pierriots jazz band, Cwmavon, Port Talbot, all set to take part in a carnival parade, early 1950s.

The cast of a pantomime staged at Cwm Y Dwr Hall, Briton Ferry, 1949.

Participants in a Nativity play staged by members of Wesley Chapel, Neath, mid-1950s.

This smartly turned out jazz band was the Afan Paraders, pictured in 1952.

Dancers at Neath Amateur Operatic Society's annual fancy dress ball at the town's Castle Hotel, January, 1951. Included are Mayor and Mayoress of Neath, Alderman and Mrs R W Perrott along with the society's president Mr H P Lloyd and Mrs Lloyd.

The Christmas pantomime staged by pupils of Brynhyfryd School, Briton Ferry, 1953.

Pupils of Cimla Infants School, Neath at their Christmas play, 1955.

Cwmavon Stewards jazz band, Port Talbot, 1954.

Mayor of the Borough of Afan, Councillor Sylvan Thomas, with young members of the Afan Paraders jazz band and their leader, Jim Needs, 1976.

Glamorgan Under 11s recorder orchestra attending a residential course at Ogmore, February, 1973. Many of its members were from Neath and Port Talbot.

Some of the cast of Neath Amateur Operatic Society's production of Call Me Madam, 1958.

Alderman Davies' Church in Wales School choir, Neath, 1958.

Cwmavon Solitairs jazz band, 1979.

The cast of a Christmas play staged at the Memorial Hall, by members of Longford Ladies Club, Neath, 1960.

Members of Melyncrythan Amateur Operatic Society ready to go on stage for its production of White Horse Inn, 1958. They are Melvyn Pearson, Brian Dennis, Colin Griffiths and John Davies.

Members of Melyncrythan Amateur Operatic Society's cast for the musical Guys and Dolls, 1960.

When it came to entertainment these three buildings provided plenty for the people of Port Talbot – and beyond. They are, from top to bottom, The Plaza cinema, Station Road, in 1985; The Odeon cinema, Bethany Square, which began and ended life under the Majestic name, 1985 and the Picturedrome cinema, Taibach, 1988.

Tonna Junior School pupils in their production of The Pied Piper, June, 1970.

Bryncoch Male Voice Choir, with conductor and organist, 1984.

Good Sports

Melyn Barbarians, Neath, 1911-1912 season.

The Sphinx Cricket XI, late 1920s.

Neath Technical School rugby XV, 1944-45.

Port Talbot County School cricket XI, 1942.

Melyn AFC, Neath, 1945-46

The Talbot Athletic Ground, Port Talbot, was the venue for a fixture between Aberavon RFC and staff at Guy's Hospital, London in 1946. These were the teams which took part, pictured with officials.

A Neath Cricket Club XI, outside the pavilion, with Fred Curtis as captain, mid-1940s.

A football team at Briton Ferry, 1946. They are pictured seated outside the former British Legion Club that stood on the site of the present Briton Ferry roundabout.

Port Talbot's Glanafan Grammar School hockey team, 1960.

A Neath Boys Club football XI outside Briton Ferry cricket pavilion, 1948.

Crowds watch an RAF gymnastic display team in action at a demonstration to commemorate the official opening of the Afan Lido Sports Centre, Port Talbot, June, 1966.

Members of Briton Ferry Steel Cricket Club on a tour to London, 1949.

Afan Lido judo club, Port Talbot, with former manager Ivor Jones, late 1960s.

Gnoll School, Neath, rugby XV, 1949-50.

Port Talbot Mayor Tom Rees starts off riders outside the Afan Lido at Aberavon seafront, on a wet first leg to the annual Five Valleys cycle race, 1970.

Skewen AFC, 1951. The picture was taken at the former Skewen Greyhound Stadium, now a housing development.

Taibach Bowls Club team, Port Talbot, 1968.

Neath YMCA rugby XV, 1951-52 with three committee members, Rees Stephens, Percy Steel and Eric Aldon.

Mayor of Port Talbot, Graham Jones, presents medals and trophies to the winners and runners up in a five-a-side football tournament at the Afan Lido sports centre, 1978.

Officials and players of Melyn Stars Football Club, Neath, early 1950s.

Cwmavon Boys Club football team, 1975.

BP Llandarcy cricketers, Neath, 1953.

Briton Ferry Cricket Club, mid-1950s.

Glanafan Comprehensive School's senior tennis team with the Port Talbot Champions Shield, June 1980.

Neath Workingmen's Club snooker team with captain Ben Griffiths, 1955.

Glanafan Comprehensive School badminton team, Port Talbot, June 1980

Glanafan Comprehensive Schools football XI, with teachers, Port Talbot, 1981.

Members of Brynhyfryd Bowling Club, Neath on their annual tour to Torquay, July, 1960.

Players and committee members of Briton Ferry Rugby Club, 1975.

Cricket spectators enjoy the action at Court Herbert, Neath, playing fields, 1962.

Glanafan Comprehensive School football team, Port Talbot, 1982.

Cefn Saeson Comprehensive School, Cimla, Neath, second year rugby XV, 1979.

A Japanese instructor-led martial arts course at the Wado-Ki Karate Club, Gwyn Hall, Neath, mid-1980s.

Actor and film star Michael Sheen is on the top right of this picture of Glanafan Comprehensive School's rugby team, pictured with teacher and coach, 1982.

Neath Golf Club officers, 1979.

Crynallt Junior School, Cimla, Neath, rugby team, 1981.

Glanafan Comprehensive School, Port Talbot, badminton team, 1981.